MW01295985

Marbella Travel Guide

Sightseeing, Hotel, Restaurant & Shopping Highlights

Richard Wright

If there are any errors or omissions in copyright acknowledgements the publisher will be pleased to insert the appropriate acknowledgement in any subsequent printing of this publication.

Table of Contents

Marbella...6
   Culture...8
   Location & Orientation 9
   Climate & When to Visit 10

Sightseeing Highlights...11
   Puerto Banus & Marina..11
   Hike Up La Concha 13
   Old Town (Casco Antiguo)......................................14
   Arabian Wall..15
   Funny Beach 16
   Golden Mile of Nueva Andalucia 17
   San Pedro de Alcántara 17
   Museum of Contemporary Spanish Engraving........18
   Flamenco Ana Maria 19
   Gibraltar Day Trip 20
   Estepona...22
   Mijas 23
   Ronda 24

Recommendations for the Budget Traveller 28
   Places to Stay 28
      La Villa Marbella..28
      La Morada Mas Hermosa Hotel.........................29
      Hotel-Apartamentos Puerta de Aduares...........29
      Vincci Seleccion Estrella del Mar.......................30
      Princesa Playa Hotel Apartamentos 30
   Places to Eat & Drink 31
      Tempora...31
      Rendez Vous...32
      Stuzzikini 32
      La Taberna del Pintxo 33
      Bar El Estrecho 33
   Places to Shop...34
      Puerto Banus Street Market...............................34
      El Corte Ingles...35
      Marina Banus...35

Centro Comercial La Cañada 36
Zoco del Sol Market 36

Marbella

The jetsetter's paradise of Marbella is located in the
province of Andalusia in the Costa del Sol region of
southern Spain. It is one of Europe's most well known
resorts for the rich and famous to "see and be seen" but
this sunny city can be enjoyed by the more budget-
conscious vacationer as well.

Marbella offers tourists a mixture of modern-day amenities mingled with the areas Moorish roots from the past. The area has a long stretch of urban yet family-friendly beaches to choose from, as well as a number of interesting museums and sights. The modern amenities in Marbella are balanced with the charm of its historic quarter with its Arab fortress standing amidst whitewashed buildings. Enjoy shopping for traditional handmade goods that include copper and brass trinkets, woven carpets, leather, wood, silver, marble, and embroidery.

Marbella's coastal location allow its visitors to enjoy a bevy of seafood dishes; the most typical is a fried fish dish that consists of mackerel, anchovies, squid, mullet, and other local types of fish. It is also very typical to see garlic soup, gazpacho, and local baked goods specific to the region.

With its warm climate, beautiful views, and Andalusian flavors, Marbella is a treat for the senses and it is a top class tourist destination in Spain.

Culture

People of Marbella are called "marbellís" or "marbellíes." Before the last half of the 20th Century, Marbella was simply a coastal village with less than 1000 residents. It wasn't until the opening of the Marbella Club in 1954 by Prince Alfonso that the area became popular with the jet setting elite when he invited nobility, movie stars, and business executives to the club. This created a tourism boom, although the area saw its fair share of corruption, especially in the 1990s. Such a rich and popular area was close to bankruptcy by the turn of the century after it was discovered that funds were misused and stolen by the government leaders. Marbella's 2007 elections have created more stability, however, and the area is still thriving.

The festival of its patron saint, Marbella, is celebrated every June with a week of activities that include Fair Day and Fair Night. A similar weeklong festival is held in October to honor the patron saint of San Pedro Alcantara. Since 2001, Marbella has been hosting the Marbella International Opera Festival every August. There is a jazz festival in June and a reggae festival in July. There is also the Spanish Film Festival, Marbella International Film Festival, and the Festival of Independent Theater. The city has both privately and publicly managed facilities for hosting these festivals and activities, including the Ingenio Cultural Center, the Auditorium of Constitution Park, the Black Box Theater, and others. There are several movie theaters showing films in the original English. There are also many neighborhood events that are celebrated throughout the summer months that are organized to encourage activity in the area.

Location & Orientation

Marbella sits on the southern coast of Spain in the province of Málaga. It occupies 44 km of coastline, sheltered by the coastal mountain range. From almost any part of the city, stunning views of both the mountains and Mediterranean Sea can be seen.

Despite being a popular tourist destination, Marbella does not have a railway station nearby. This means that renting a car or using the Intercity Bus is necessary. The airport closest to Marbella is Pablo Ruiz Picasso Airport in Málaga, which has rental car service and bus service to Marbella and the other cities along the Costa del Sol.

Renting a car and driving to Marbella from the Malaga airport is quite easy. From the rental car station, leave the airport by following the signs that lead you to the A-7 towards Cadiz-Algeciras. The drive takes a little over a half of an hour.

If you prefer to let someone else do the driving while on your vacation, there is an efficient bus service accessible from the airport's Terminal 3 bus stop at the front of the terminal. Buses are run by the Portillo bus company, and drop you off at the Marbella bus station in under an hour.

Climate & When to Visit

Marbella has a very mild climate with an average temperature of 66°F (19°C). Its 320 days of sunshine annually makes it a pleasant place to visit throughout the year, despite the colder winter months between December and February. It is protected on its northern side by the coastal mountains of the Cordillera Penibética range, where it is common to see snow on its highest peaks.

Due to Marbella's reputation as a popular tourist destination, the summer months between June and September are the most congested. However, the beginning of June can be quite comfortable, with more hotel vacancies and room to breathe. Many people say that the best time to go is during the last two weeks of September when the weather is still nice, the large crowds are less common, and the Spanish restaurant and hotel owners have returned from vacations of their own.

Sightseeing Highlights

Puerto Banus & Marina

29660 Marbella, Málaga, Spain

Be sure to visit the most famous marina in the Marbella area and the idea of developer José Banus which is Puerto Banus. It was Monaco's Prince Rainier and his wife, Grace Kelly who were responsible for it attaining its celebrity status after opening it in 1970. It is now a "must see" attraction when visiting Marbella.

Puerto Banus is a ritzy marina with room for hundreds of vessels, spanning 37 acres (15 hectares), but you do not need to lead a lifestyle of the rich and famous to appreciate it. Allow yourself to mingle amongst the elite society of yacht owners as if you are one of them, even if only for just a day.

If travelling to Puerto Banus by car, park in the Antonio Banderas Square. The port is directly across the street. You will see parking spaces at the marina, but do not attempt to park there. It is closed to traffic unless you have a yacht docked there or work at the marina. The square is a good meeting point and rest stop with its numerous parking spots, coffee shop, and outdoor play area for the kids.

Once you are ready to visit the port, there is plenty to do besides perusing the luxury yachts. Keep in mind that it gets crowded during the summer months, as it is the place to see and be seen. Arriving by 10:00 a.m. is a good time in order to enjoy the scenery before it fills up.

Puerto Banus is also an upscale shopping area with names like Dolce & Gabbana and Louis Vuitton. Smaller boutiques, nightclubs, bars and restaurants line the streets of the port as well. The nightlife scene is energetic and brings in a lot of money to the area. Puerto Banus has something for everyone no matter what time of day it is.

Hike Up La Concha

(From Juanar – Sierra Blanca, s/n 29610 Ojén, Málaga)

Nature lovers will love hiking up La Concha, the landmark mountain of 1200 meters (3937 feet) that sets the backdrop for Marbella. On a clear day, hikers can see all the way across the sea to Gibraltar in North Africa. It is a romantic spot to watch the sunset, if you are brave enough to hike back down the mountain in the dark.

In Spanish, La Concha means "shell" and, yes, the mountain is shaped like a shell. It is located within the southernmost part of the Sierra Blancas and is accessible via two main routes. One route starts in Istan. This is the steepest and most demanding of the two. The second route is easier but takes longer to navigate and starts at the El Refugio de Juanar. This is the recommended route.

To get to Refugio de Juanar, take the A-355 as if you are headed to the Centro Comercial La Cañada (the shopping center). There is a roundabout just before the center. Instead of turning towards the center, head straight, towards Ojen. Once at Juanar, there are a few routes to viewing points from which to choose. One is the Mirador del Corzo with an easy 500 meter (1640 foot) walk to a viewing point. Another is the Mirador del Macho Montès: an easy but longer route. The route is less than one mile long (1.3 km) and leads through olive groves to a viewing point that provides breathtaking views across Marbella. Another option is the Cruz de Juanar, a bit further up and an hour's walk to and from the viewing point.

Although the hikes are rather easy, be aware that you should always bring enough water, sunscreen, and a mobile phone. The number for emergency services is 112. There are professional guides who can lead you up the mountain safely, should you feel more comfortable that way.

Old Town (Casco Antiguo)

Maintaining the same look as it did in the 16th century, behind the ancient city walls, is Old Town Marbella – also known as Casco Antiguo. Marbella's two historical suburbs, Barrio Alto and Barrio Nuevo, sit within the perimeters of Old Town, behind the ancient city walls. After a Franciscan convent located to the Barrio Alto suburb, it became known as the San Francisco neighborhood. It is within this part of the Old Town where Marbella's history throughout the years if visibly displayed. Architectural styles from the Castilian Renaissance, as well as Gothic and Baroque styles can be seen here; in the form of the town hall, the Mayor's house, the Chapel of Santiago, Capilla de San Juan de Dios, and more.

The Parque Arroyo de la Represa separates the Barrio Nuevo from the Barrio Alto. This newer part of the Old Town lacks any monumental buildings but still has the same layout as it did centuries ago, as well as much of its original charm.

Casco Antiguo is a beautiful place to simply stroll around and stop for a meal or drink at one of the numerous cafes. It is also full of little shops, but keep in mind that most are closed on Sundays during the autumn, winter, and spring months. Plazo de los Naranjos (Orange Square) with its abundance of orange trees is a historic and gorgeous place to sit and relax under the orange blossoms. This square was the center of political and commercial life for hundreds of years and still has its original 15th century chapel, Renaissance-style fountain, and impressive mansions.

Arabian Wall

Visible from the Old Town are the walls from the ancient Arab Castle that protected its Arabian royalty centuries ago. The best way to see them is by making your way from Orange Square (Plazo de los Naranjos) via Trinidad Street. You will pass a row of small houses before encountering the castle walls. The wall continues down to Portada Street before disappearing. If Spanish history is not of much interest to you, you may find it unnecessary to make a special trip to the wall, as there really is not much else to see. However, it deserves mentioning as most tourists find themselves wondering, "What is that giant wall?"

Funny Beach

184 Carretera Nacional 340, Marbella 29600
http://funnybeach.com/?lang=en
(+34) 95 282 3359

The water and sand are some of the main draws to Funny Beach, but it is not only a beach. This fun park is situated on the coast just after you enter Marbella, under the arched entrance sign. There is something for people of all ages; including trampolines, bounce houses, go-karts, video games, miniature golf, darts, and a mechanical bull. There is also a separate play area for little ones. An onsite restaurant offers family-friendly buffet service. The best feature may be that admission to the park is free. You do, however, have to pay for each attraction separately.

Funny Beach also offers a variety of open water activities such as water scooter (jet ski) rental at a cost of 50€ for 15 minutes. You can also try parasailing for up to three people (50€ for one person, 80€ for two, and 100€ for three. Also, at 20€ for 15 minutes, you can do "trawling," which involves being pulled on a tube by boat. If you are looking for something more relaxing, consider the pedal boats at a cost of 20€ for an entire hour.

Funny Beach is open every day except Monday from 11:30 a.m. until 9:30 p.m.

Golden Mile of Nueva Andalucia

The Golden Mile is actually not a mile at all. It is a stretch of four miles that starts at Puerto Banús and heads into the Nueva Andalucia neighborhood of Marbella. This is home to the most glamorous homes in the area and one of these homes is the Palace of King Fahd. There are also some noteworthy hotels where the rich and famous stay when visiting the area.

The glamorous neighborhood of Nueva Andalucía was developed during the 1960s, when there was a boost in tourism. The magnificent views of both the coast and the mountains were such a draw for the wealthy tourists that many of them ended up buying property there, and the size of the homes reflect the wealth that was once thrown upon the region.

The Golden Mile is an example of what defines Marbella's appeal. It is worth a drive or a stroll if you have time in your itinerary.

San Pedro de Alcántara

Located a short 6 mile (10 km) drive west of Marbella is San Pedro de Alcántara, where you can escape the crowds of Marbella and sample the most traditional Spanish town that remains on the Costa del Sol. San Pedro de Alcántara is very well kept – clean and quiet – with beautiful gardens and a centrally located shopping area. Although its traditional Spanish style remains, a newer "Nueva Alcántara" showcases the newer developments taking place with a new promenade and beaches similar to Marbella but on a much smaller scale.

Two 19th century industrial buildings stand in the middle of San Pedro de Alcántara: the sugar mill, which is now home to the Ingenio Cultural Center; and the Trapiche de Guadaiza.

San Pedro is also home to the ancient Roman baths of Las Bóvedas (the Domes). It is believed that the building that houses the baths was built in the 3rd century by the Romans before an earthquake destroyed them in 365 AD. To access the ruins, head toward Guadalmina Beach, as it is only 10 meters away from it. You may see signs that read, Termas Romanas de Guadalmina (Roman Baths of Guadalmina). There are guided tours of the ruins offered by appointment at noon on Tuesdays, Thursdays, and Saturdays by calling 952-781-360. Tours are free.

Museum of Contemporary Spanish Engraving

Calle Hospital de Bazán, s/n, 29601 Marbella
http://mgec.es/
(+34) 952 76 57 41

The Museo del Grabado Español Contemporáneo
(Museum of Contemporary Spanish Engraving) is located
in the old 16th century Bazan Hospital in the middle of
Old Town. It houses contemporary prints by some of the
most famous 20th century artists in Spain, such as Miró
and Picasso.

The museum also displays temporary exhibitions. Guided
tours allow visitors to learn more about these exhibitions
as well as the building's rich history on Tuesdays through
Fridays. It is open from 10:00 a.m. until 2:00 p.m. on
Saturdays and Mondays. On Tuesdays through Fridays, it
is open from 10:00 a.m. until 7:00 p.m. The museum is
closed on Sundays. The cost is €3.

Flamenco Ana Maria

Plaza Santo Cristo, 4, 29609 Marbella, Málaga, Spain
(+34) 634 36 65 78
http://www.flamencoanamaria.com/english/

To truly get the true Spanish experience, a Flamenco
show should be added to your itinerary.

This Andalucian dancing tradition involves women dressed in colorful "gypsy" style dresses performing their signature, dramatic dance moves. Nobody really knows where the traditions of flamenco music and dance originated. The term, "Flamenco," started to be used during the 18th century when Flamenco schools started operating in Cadiz. But the stories and folklore surrounding the passionate art form started hundreds of years ago and were survived by Spanish grandmothers who would pass them down to their children.

Tablao Flamenco Ana Maria has been hosting Flamenco shows since 1991. If you would rather be a part of the scene instead of a spectator, consider taking one of their classes. Flamenco Ana Maria is open daily from 9:00 p.m. until 3:00 a.m.

Gibraltar Day Trip

The British territory of Gibraltar is a 2.6 square mile (6.8 square kilometer) area that borders Spain to the north and juts out into the Mediterranean Sea. Its Rock of Gibraltar is a popular tourist destination who visit to see fabulous sea views and the famous apes. Gibraltar (and nearby Algeciras) acts as a departure point for those wanting to leave the European mainland and head across the Mediterranean to Northern Africa's Morocco.

Located a short 45 minutes by car from Marbella, a day trip to Gibraltar is both easy and worthwhile. From Marbella, simply take N 340, the main highway, towards Algeciras. After passing Sotogrande, watch for signs for the Gibraltar (La Linea) exit and head in the direction of the sea.

There are some important things you will need to know when visiting Gibraltar. First and foremost, passports are needed in order to enter the British territory. (If you are European, an identity card will suffice.) You will need a passport to reenter Spain, however, and if you plan on continuing your trip on to Morocco. Officially the currency here is not the Euro but it is accepted in practice. You can exchange your money for Gibraltar pounds or pounds sterling to get better rates in the shops. Most shops are open from 9:00 a.m. until 7:30 p.m. on weekdays, half days on Saturdays, and closed on Sundays.

If you are not up to driving to Gibraltar, consider checking with your hotel to see if they provide a tour from Marbella. Otherwise, a coach trip or taxi is a good idea, and the drivers tend to share useful information about the destination. Coach trips can be booked ahead of time and take visitors all over the "island" (which is actually a peninsula). The average price for such a tour is £15 per person. The drawbacks are that you are limited to the group's schedule and itinerary.

If you are looking for a more personal trip, consider a taxi tour which allows you to explore on your own terms and at your own pace. A taxi tour can take you to the entrance to the tunnels and caves of Gibraltar.

There is also a cable car that can take you to the top of the rock of Gibraltar but it does not include the entrance fee. Still, for the £6 one-way and £7 return, it is a low price to pay for such amazing views.

While in Gibraltar, there is more to do than simply gaze at the large "rock." Consider visiting the apes den in the nature reserve – home to the Barbary Apes which can be seen living in their natural habitat, out in the wild. There are several caves, tunnels, and places to explore; including St. Michael's cave - a stunning grotto over 300 meters above sea level with its stalagmites and stalactites. Be very careful that the apes do not run away with anything loosely carried including sunglasses, hats and camera cases.

Estepona

A 30-minute drive on the AP7 will take you to the charming town of Estepona. Estepona is a fishing port and this is reflected in the menus of its restaurants. Here you can watch the daily auctions for the areas diverse variety of seafood. Like any city on the Costa del Sol, the beaches of Estepona are the main attractions. Christ Beach (Playa del Cristo) is about five minutes west of the Port of Estepona. It is a smaller beach with lifeguards and a couple beachfront restaurants. A popular nudist beach, Costa Natura, is also just west of Estepona and was the first naturist beach in Spain. Just a couple minutes east of Estepona is La Rada Beach, spanning a massive 1.5 km (just under one mile).

Selwo Aventura in Estepona is a nature park and wild animal park with approximately 2000 animals from over 200 different species, living in a setting very close to their natural habitats. The park offers photographic African safaris via all-terrain vehicles to its guests. After visiting the lions, tigers, apes, and bears; guests end their safari at the highest point in the park – Africa's Window. It is here where the coastline and Gibraltar are visible. For more great views of the park, visit the Path of the Hanging Bridges. There are many other attractions and exhibits at the park, as well as onsite shops and restaurants.

The park is located at Autovia Costa del Sol Km 162.5 and is open from 10 a.m. until 7 p.m. Prices for those ages 10-65 are 24,50€, and 17€ for those ages 3-9. If you are without a car, there is a bus that you can reserve on Wednesdays and Fridays that picks up its guests at various stops in Estepona. You can reserve it by calling 902 19 04 82.

Mijas

A popular town to visit on the Costa del Sol is Mijas. Mijas actually consists of Mijas Pueblo and Mijas Costa. Mijas Pueblo is a typical whitewashed Andalusian village perched above sea level on the side of a mountain. The areas just outside of Mijas Pueblo on the coast are called Mijas Costa. The most populous part of Mijas is Las Lagunas, which is integrated with Fuengirola. Fuengirola offers bus service to Mijas regularly: take bus number 122. If you are looking to visit the beaches, you can also stay in Fuengirola, just 15 km from Mijas Pueblo.

From Mijas Pueblo, you can see amazing views of the North African coast, Gibraltar, the Atlas Mountains, and much of the rest of the Costa del Sol. This is also where you can find the Mijas traditional bullring and the town plaza where small donkey trolleys offer trips around the village. Rock climbing and golfing are also popular in Mijas Pueblo.

If you have children, or simply want to escape the heat yourself, it may be wise to blow off some steam at the aquatic park (Parque Acuatico de Mijas). From adventurous slides to wave pools, there is plenty to do for all ages. The prices are 23 euros for adults, 17 euros for 8 to 12 year-olds, and 12 euros for 3 to 7 year-olds. After 2:30 p.m., there is a 30% discount and the park is less crowded.

There is also a horse track in Mijas called, Hipodromo de Mijas at Urbanisación El Chaparral (+34 952 592 700). When racing season is over in the United Kingdom, a lot of the horse owners bring their horses to Mijas to continue racing. It is the largest complex on the Costa del Sol and remains open year-round. If you are traveling with your dog, the Hipodromo offers a unique dog hotel so that you can enjoy the races without worrying about leaving your pet alone for the day. There is also a residential hotel on the premise if you care to stay longer. There are bars and restaurants on site, as well as a souvenir shop and play area for the kids. Parking is free. On Sundays, the racetrack offers a "rastro" market with vendors selling second-hand items. It is open to the public from 9:00 a.m. until 2:00 p.m.

The racetrack opens at 10:30 a.m. with races starting at 11:30. The entrance fee is 5 € for adults. Children aged under 18 can enter free of charge.

Ronda

Tucked away in a deep gorge is the town of Ronda which makes for a pleasant day trip from Marbella. It has a more relaxed atmosphere than most of the other touristy places on the nearby Costa del Sol, but can still get crowded with tourists on coach tours, especially in summer. There are no trains connecting Marbella to Ronda, but there is a bus service. The drive takes about one and a half hours.

Ronda is a small town that is easily navigable by foot and there is plenty to see and do. The Puente Nuevo is the scenic bridge over the gorge of el Tajo that actually has a small museum in side of it. It was finished in 1793 and spans 100 meters 328 feet) from top to bottom. To give you a better idea of its height, it is the size of a 30-story building. For impressive photo shots of the bridge, consider a walk to the bottom of the gorge.

The main street in town is Calle la Bola. Bola is the Spanish word for "ball," a nickname earned for the street when the town's residents rolled a giant snowball down the street after a heavy snowfall. This is the "main drag" for strolling and shopping.

One of Spain's oldest bullrings, Plaza de Toros, is located in Ronda. There is a museum inside with an admission charge of €6. Next to the bullring is La Alameda, a park with plenty of shade-providing trees and room to walk around and take in the views.

Ronda has an "old town" called, La Ciudad, behind the new bridge that crosses the gorge. Like many other "old towns," it is a charming maze of narrow streets. This is where you can find the Church of Santa Maria la Mayor as well as the Palacio de Mondragon. The church is a Gothic-style cathedral with elements of Baroque and Rococo inside as well. The Palacio de Mondragon used to be a Moorish palace. Now it is a place to enjoy beautiful gardens and views as well as the small museum inside.

While taking in the sights of the old town, head east, down the hill to the old bridge – Puente Viejo. This bridge was used to cross the Tajo gorge before the conception of the newer bridge. Nearby is a beautiful arch called, Arco de Felipe V, named after Phillip the Fifth.

If you are a fan of wine, consider a visit to Interpretation Center of Ronda Wine on Calle Gonzalez Campos No. 2. (+34) 95 287 9735. It is an old winery and an interesting wine museum as well. It is open from 10 a.m. until 8 p.m.

Recommendations for the Budget Traveller

Places to Stay

La Villa Marbella

Calle Principe 10 Old Historic Town, 29600 Marbella
(+34) 952 76 62 20
http://www.lavillamarbella.com/

Averaging 150€ per night, depending upon the season, La Villa Marbella is a great place to stay while visiting Marbella. Its location is ideal with Orange Square only a three minute walk away and Puerto Banus only a ten minute walk.

This is a romantic hotel that offers free breakfast to its guests, as well as complementary WiFi and laundry facilities. Guests can also enjoy the bar and lounge as well as the scenic rooftop terrace. There is a babysitter service as well as airport transfers.

La Morada Mas Hermosa Hotel

Calle Montenebros 16 Casco Antiguo, 29601 Marbella
+34 952 92 44 67
http://www.lamoradamashermosa.com/

La Morada Mas Hermosa is a beautiful hotel located in
the Old Town of Marbella. It is situated on a pedestrian
only street, and you can park in the nearby Mercado
Municipal, only a 200 meter walk from the hotel. Guests
can get a breakfast basket delivered to their rooms, or
take their breakfast in the common area. Rooms average
100€ per night depending on the type of room and time of
year. The hotel also offers airport transfers.

Hotel-Apartamentos Puerta de Aduares

C/ Aduar, 18, 29601 Marbella
(+34) 952 82 13 12
http://www.puertadeaduares.com/

This centrally located hotel offers roomy apartment-like
accommodations on a budget. Averaging 100€, the
"rooms" are a steal with their kitchenettes and terraces or
balconies. Parking is free. The beaches are only a five
minute walk from the hotel; which sits on a quiet,
residential street. The owners are friendly as well.

Vincci Seleccion Estrella del Mar

Carretera Nacional 340 Km 191, Las Chapas, 29604
Marbella
(+34) 951 05 39 70
http://www.vinccihoteles.com

This is a resort with every amenity you can imagine
averaging 150€ per night. The resort is located just besides
the sea and has beach access as well as an outdoor
swimming pool. It is 5 miles (8 km) from the center of
Marbella in the area of Elviria Las Chapas. Its 137 rooms
and suites reflect a modern Mediterranean style with a bit
of Arab influence. This is the hotel to book if you are on a
slight budget but want to feel like high society.

Princesa Playa Hotel Apartamentos

 Paseo Maritimo, s/n, 29600 Marbella
(+34) 952 82 09 44
http://www.hotelprincesaplaya.com/en/index.htm

The Princesa Playa Hotel Apartamentos is a value,
averaging 75€ per night and located right on the beach
with only a five minute walk to the Old Town. It offers 64
rooms and 36 apartments as well as a restaurant, a terrace
bar, and an outdoor swimming pool. It was completely
refurbished in 2006, but is still an older hotel; so if you are
looking for something very modern, you might want to
consider looking elsewhere. Still, it is a great value and
spotlessly clean.

Places to Eat & Drink

Tempora

Tetuan 9a, 29601 Marbella
(+34) 95 285 7933

Tempora is a newer restaurant in the Old Town of
Marbella with a name that means, "season" in Spanish.
Despite its youth, this quaint establishment has already
garnered the respect and adoration of both locals and
tourists alike. The owner's philosophy is to cook with
fresh, seasonal ingredients in order to prepare and serve
dishes of the highest possible quality.

Every day, Chef Abraham Garrote Costa accompanies
owner, Andrés Perdiguero to the local market in search
for the ingredients that will suit their menu for the day.
Since they use only the produce that is "in season," you
will most likely find a different menu with each visit. To
find the restaurant, find the horse fountain across from
Parque de Alameda. Once at the fountain, Tetuan is the
first street on your right. Tempora is on the left side of the
street, in the middle of the block.

Prices are not extravagant and you can expect to pay an
average of 20€ per entrée. Reservations are accepted.

Rendez Vous

Avenida del Prado Nueva Andalucia, 29660 Marbella
(+34) 952 813 912
http://rendezvous-marbella.com/

Rendez Vous is a French bistro located in the heart of
Marbella. The owners, Mikael and Céline, are known for
their traditional French dishes and their macarons. Do not
be intimidated by its fancy interior. It is very budget
friendly while remaining classy. Rendez Vous is open on
Tuesdays through Sundays from 9 a.m. until 5 p.m. for
breakfast and lunch. On Sundays, they offer a brunch
service. Every Friday, from 7 p.m. until 9 p.m., the
restaurant offers champagne tasting paired with some of
Chef Mikael's dishes.

Stuzzikini

c/Alderete 5, 29600 Marbella
(+34) 952 775 994
http://www.stuzzikini.com/

Stuzzikini is the project of Chef Robert, who has spent his
formative cooking years in Italy, Spain, and England. He
serves Italian food that makes people think they are in
Sardinia. The dishes are unique but still carry a trace of
their homelands. Atmosphere at Stuzzikini is relaxed but
adheres to a high attention to detail that includes
charming Italian music.

Stuzzikini is open daily except for Tuesdays, from 7:00 p.m. until close. Reservations are recommended.

La Taberna del Pintxo

Avenida Miguel Cano, 7, 29600 Marbella
(+34) 952 829 321
http://www.latabernadelpintxo.com/

The Basque regions equivalent of "tapas" is a "pinxto," which is this Basque restaurants specialty. La Taberna del Pintxo offer two categories of pinxtos; cold and hot. The cold pinxtos can be purchased at the bar while the hot pinxtos are served at the table. Their cuisine includes flavors from both the north and south of Spain as well as ingredients of the best quality. They are also known for serving good Spanish wine.

Bar El Estrecho

Calle San Lazaro 12 Old Town, 29601 Marbella
(+34) 95 277 0004
http://www.barelestrecho.es/

Open since 1954, this tapas restaurant serves traditional Spanish cuisine in a charming atmosphere. It is slightly hidden, in a narrow alley in old town, but this should not discourage you from looking for it. Service is consistently friendly and accommodating. Prices range from $5 to $15.

Places to Shop

Considering the fact that Marbella is one of those destinations where people go to see and be seen, one of the most popular things to shop for in Marbella is clothing. Although it has its share of high-end shops, it offers its visitors fashionable European style apparel at rates which are actually more reasonable than many other European cities.

If you are looking for something in particular, Marbella's megastores like El Corte Ingles will not disappoint. But the best way to find hidden treasures at bargain prices is simply to stroll through town and stop at one of the many local merchants or street markets.

Puerto Banus Street Market

Boulevard de La Fama (parking at Centro Plaza mall on calle Camilo Jose Cela)

Just a short walk from the centre of Puerto Banus and located near the bullring is the Saturday Puerto Banus street market. This is a great place to buy souvenirs and just about anything else you can imagine. Start at the bullring and head down to the port as you browse the spices, clothes, vegetables, and furniture. Parking can be congested, so be sure to arrive early or late. Although it opens at 9 a.m., many stalls aren't ready until 10 a.m. It closes at 2 p.m.

El Corte Ingles

Calle Ramón Areces in Puerto Banus
(+34) 952 909 990
http://www.elcorteingles.es/

El Corte Inglés is a must-see department store in Marbella and is the largest shopping chain in all of Spain and all of Europe. It is here that you can find everything you need, including brands from the best names in fashion. There is also a supermarket (Hipercor), optician, and travel agency.

El Corte Ingles is open Monday through Saturday from 10:00 a.m. to 10:00 p.m. in the winter and daily from 10:30 a.m. to 10:30 p.m. in the summer.

Marina Banus

Calle Ramon Areces, 29600
(+34) 952 906 544
http://www.marinabanus.com/

If El Corte Ingles is too overwhelming for you, Marina Banus may be more your style. Simply head across the road from El Corte Ingles to reach this smaller, more budget friendly mall. Within the mall are approximately 30 stores as well as restaurants and a hair salon. It is also family-friendly with a play area for toddlers. The mall is open Monday through Saturday from 10:00 a.m. to 10:00 p.m. in the winter and daily from 10:30 a.m. to 10:30 p.m. in the summer.

Centro Comercial La Cañada

Carretera Ojén, Marbella 29602
(+34) 95 286 5076

The Centro Comercial La Cañada is similar to Marina Banus in size and has everything you would expect from a mall. The difference is mostly in its ample parking spaces and that it is less crowded than the malls on Puerto Banus. The shops include Armand Basi, Mango, Zara, and Dorothy Perkins and there is a large Alcampo supermarket.

The Centro Comercial La Cañada is open daily from 10 a.m. until 10 p.m. (except Sundays).

Zoco del Sol Market

Plaza Antonio Banderas, Puerto Banus

The Zoco del Sol is an open-air market that occurs daily during the summertime. During the rest of the year, it is open only on Saturdays. Situated on Plaza Antonio Banderas (named after the famous movie actor who was born in the area) between the El Corte Ingles Shopping Center and the port, this market has 25 stalls that sell unique art, vintage clothing, jewelry, fragrances, and glass. Park in the lot under the central square and walk the short distance to the market. It is open from 11 a.m. until midnight during the summer and from 10 a.m. until 4 p.m. on Saturdays during the rest of the year.

Made in United States
North Haven, CT
15 March 2023

34088834R00022